King Solitaire's Big Banquet

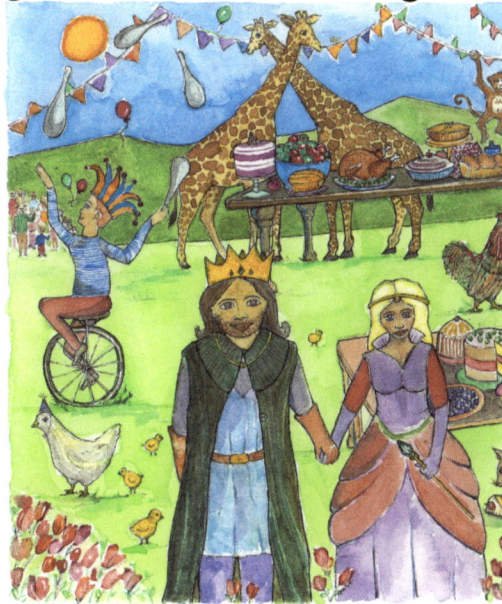

Lydia du Toit

My husband, Francois, and I live in South Africa. We have been married for 41 years.
We are blessed with four amazing children and three grandchildren,
with another one on the way!
I think my passion for story telling started in my early childhood.
We lived like gypsies then, in a caravan, and traveled crisscross our beautiful country,
wherever my Papa's work would take him. This was long before TV.
So, we invented our own stories, and created places in our imagination - places yet to be discovered.
We would tell them around the campfire, or listen to Mamma's wonderful tales when she tucked us into bed,
taking us with her to Neverland.
C.S. Lewis and his Narnia stories, as well as Elizabeth Goudge's books, are some of my favorites.
There is a wonder-world waiting to be discovered in every young mind and I wish that reading this story
will awaken an understanding of a limitless love and a life full of adventure.

Our son, Christo, made the illustrations. You can see more of his wonderful work here: @christo_francois_art
This book is dedicated to our dear friends Patrick and Pamela Emery

King Solitaire woke up one morning with a brilliant idea in his head, he was so excited and could not wait to share it with Queen Beatrice, who was still fast asleep in her lovely big bed.

At last, when she awoke, he jumped onto the bed with joy.

"Oh I have a brilliant idea, you must listen to this" and he proceeded to tell her of the big banquet and the riddle which he had dreamt of and now wanted to plan with her.

This is how our story began.

So the King wrote a very smart invitation on his very smart paper with his very smart signature on.

This is what it said...

EVERYONE IS INVITED!!!

Please come and join Queen Beatrice and me at the castle for a riddle and a feast.

I have ordered the most delicious food and the best music you have ever heard – a festival is prepared with so much jolly you will never ever forget it.

However, before entry is granted, you must prove that you are the best.

No matter what you are the best at – but the best you have to be to come dine with me!

The winner, you see, will open the gates, for all is free.

Get ready and prepare and come to this fair.

Signed:

King Solitaire &

Queen Beatrice

The cavalry mounted their horses and galloped off, clickety clack, to the four corners of the land, carrying this most magnificent invitation. Also, the sailors rigged the sails of their fastest ships and sailed across the waters, swoosh swash swish, all prepared with the magnificent banquet invitation.

Oh, the news spread quickly, near and far! The excitement was tangible and everywhere people began preparing for this great event and most intriguing riddle. Some were thinking and others reasoning, others just dreaming! Some were running, some swimming, some doing tricks and others brewing a fix.

As the days progressed people started arriving at the King's castle. Big wooden gates and horsemen guarded the entrance and at the bottom of the gate sat the King and Queen, all dressed up, excitedly examining everyone who presented themselves.

First was Swift William – oh everyone knew he was the fastest man in the land. King Solitaire asked him to give some account of his fast running legs. Swift William proceeded to tell the King everything. How he could outrun a mule and even a fox. On a good day he could run from one end of the land to the other!

King Solitaire was very impressed, but of course he had to first inspect what was written in The Book of Stars. Every astonishing and amazing, as well us every unremarkable and uninspiring, person or event was jotted down in this great book! Meticulously he paged through it, until he found someone that had actually outrun Swift William.

Someone who could run as fast as a hippopotamus! How did they possibly know that, you may ask? Well, as the story goes, Cleopas was walking on the banks of the great Euphrates River early one morning and was surprised by an angry hippopotamus!

The hippopotamus was particularly miserable because of such toothache and so chased Cleopas all the way home. The King was sad to inform dear Swift William that there actually was someone faster than him, so he had to leave and go back home.

Then came Hilarious Henrietta. She was the funniest lady in all the land. There was not a man or woman that could resist her jokes — even if they bit on their lips and clinched their teeth, trying hard not to laugh — they always ended up in stitches. She proceeded to tell the King and the Queen some of her jokes and they laughed so much, the King was bouncing on his throne!

He then took The Book of Stars and started paging through it slowly, when he found the heading 'Jesters'.

Alas, there he found a jester who told such funny jokes that he once made a prince fall right off his horse! So, they had to tell Hilarious Henrietta that she was not the funniest person in the land! And again, a great sigh was heard in the crowd as they realized that their next hopeful candidate to open the gate also failed!

Then it was the turn of Strong Silvanus. Oh my goodness, he was so strong he could pick up a horse, can you believe it? He wanted to prove to King Solitaire how strong he was and promptly lifted up the King and the Queen together, in his arms.

But they did not enjoy being picked up and swung around like that, so the King sternly ordered Strong Silvanus to put them down immediately.

He then took The Book of Stars out and began to page through it, looking for the strongest man ever.

He found a few that were even stronger than Strong Silvanus, who was also sent on his way.

By now there was a long queue of contestants standing at the castle gates. The sounds of joyous music from behind the castle walls and the smell of all the delightful food drifted over to them and made them even more determined to get in and partake in the feast.

Skinny Winney had the Queen in tears; she was so skinny that one could almost see right through her!

It was quite tough for King Solitaire to tell her that he actually found someone in The Book of Stars that was even skinnier than her:

Little Less Than Nothing, a very skinny lad, whom even a child could lift up with one hand!

Then Big Man Moodley came and stood in front of the King, shaking and sweating. He was so large and exhausted from the long walk to get to the castle.

King Solitaire was quite sure that Big Man Moodley was the biggest man he had ever seen.

However, in The Book of Stars there was a man that was so big, ten children holding hands could make a circle around his belly – oh my goodness, how big is that?

The people stood for days, all of them – the wisest and the silliest, the fastest and the slowest, the least to the most noble, the richest and the poorest – all were turned down by the King because there was just always someone in The Book of Stars that outshone them.

Queen Beatrice was so sad and anxious – she thought that they would be the only two at this incredible banquet. Is there then no one that can open the gates to the banquet? Just then she looked up and there, standing in front of them, was a boy she recognized.

"Young man," said the King, "why are you here again? I have certainly seen your face before."

"I know, dear King Solitaire and Queen Beatrice, I am Jonagold, the boy who could eat more apples than you have ever seen before! But you also disqualified me because you found someone in your book that was better than me, so I went home.

My parents were so disappointed that they had me sleep outside with the animals that night.

Then I too had a dream, just as you did, dear King Solitaire. I couldn't wait to come and tell you why I am the best, and that I have the answer to your riddle, which will open the banquet for everyone!"

"Oh, dear lad, you had better tell me immediately," the King commanded him. "What are you the best at, may I know?"

"I am the best me", said Jonagold.

"Go ahead, dear King Solitaire, page through your Book of Stars from beginning to end, you will never find anyone who is a better, more amazing Jonagold than me!"

King Solitaire took The Book of Stars and started paging from beginning to end and from end to beginning.

The Queen was getting so excited; she moved to the edge of her throne and whispered in the King's ear, "Oh, my darling, it seems someone has solved your riddle!"

"Yes, I know" he whispered back. "I am so overjoyed!"

Indeed, it did not matter how many times King Solitaire paged through The Book of Stars, he could not find a better, more amazing Jonagold in all the world!

Then he began to shout out the good news.

And soon it spread everywhere.

"Come enjoy the feast, everyone.

The gates are now open for all!"

From near and far all the people big and small ran into the castle grounds for the feast to begin.

They were singing and dancing with jolly joy.

The End

mirrorWORD

For all who read this story
You have no competition to be you
You are valued and unique
And you are loved
Lydia

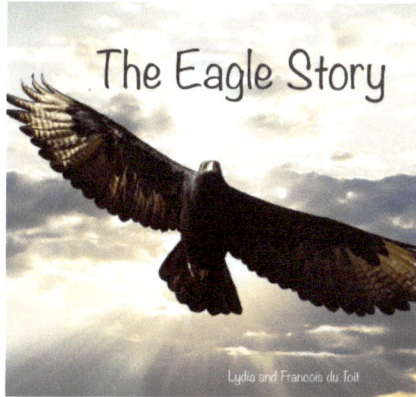

The Eagle Story

Lydia and Francois du Toit

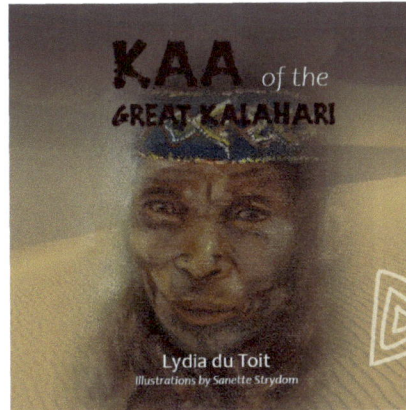

KAA of the GREAT KALAHARI

Lydia du Toit

Illustrations by Sanette Strydom

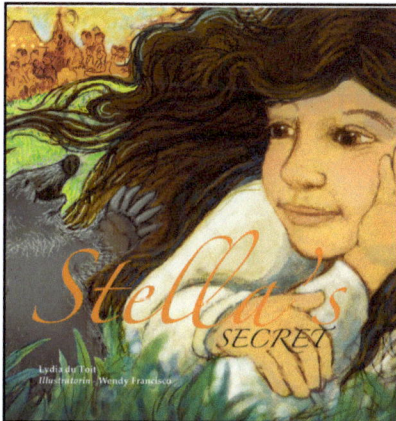

Stella's SECRET

Lydia du Toit
Illustrations Wendy Francisco

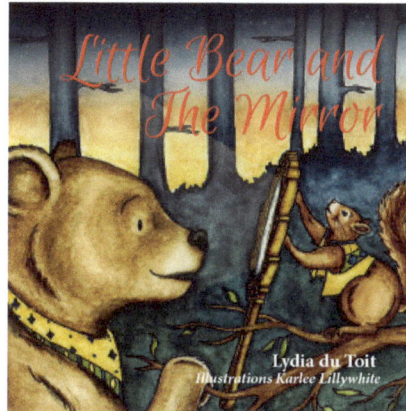

Little Bear and The Mirror

Lydia du Toit
Illustrations Karlee Lillywhite

For more amazing children's books by Lydia,
- The Eagle Story, KAA of the Great Kalahari
- Stella's Secret,
- The Little Bear and The Mirror,
also translated into Afrikaans, German and Spanish
visit our website
www.morrorword.net

www.ingramcontent.com/pod-product-compliance
Lightning Source LLC
Chambersburg PA
CBHW042121040426
42449CB00003B/143